The Literary Genius of Lil Wayne: The case for Lil Wayne to be counted among Shakespeare and Dylan © 2015 by Kreston Kent

Kreston Kent
c/o Keel Publications
P.O. Box 160155
Austin, TX 78716
info@krestonkent.com
www.krestonkent.com

Published October, 2014
2nd Edition May, 2015

ISBN-13: 978-1502969873
ISBN-10: 1502969874

# The Literary Genius of Lil Wayne

*The case for Lil Wayne to be
counted among Shakespeare and Dylan*

by Professor Kreston Kent

## About the Author

Kreston Kent, an exact contemporary of Dwayne Michael Carter, Jr. (aka Lil Wayne or Weezy) studied political science alongside Wayne at the University of Houston in the Spring of 2005. While Mr. Carter left academia to pursue his music, Kent continued on to graduate school  at the University of Virginia en route to his future professorship. In addition to studying politics and philosophy, Kent studied classical composition at the Moore's School of Music and wrote a thesis analyzing musical forms and structures in the speeches of Abraham Lincoln.

A recipient of the Earhart Foundation Fellowship, Professor Kent has taught at the University of Virginia and Piedmont Virginia Community College, and college preparatory schools, instructing politics, philosophy and mathematics.

## About the Lyrics

All lyrics contained herein were transcribed directly from audio recordings by the author. Many of the songs quoted were audio files publicly released for free online by the copyright holders. All are used solely for the purpose of criticism and comment and are quoted minimally to make analytical points about the literary devices employed.

# Preface to the 2nd Edition

*The All Out Show*

Shortly after the release of the first edition, I spoke to
Rude Jude on Sirius/XM Shade 45's "The All Out
Show." After discussing some of the essential points of
the book, we took questions from callers, some of
whom were adamant that Lil Wayne wasn't doing
anything a dozen rappers before him hadn't done.
They challenged me by asking to what extent I had
delved into other rappers' lyrics, to which I responded
that every time I had tried to analyze other rappers'
lyrics in the same way, there just wasn't anything of
comparable literary merit to analyze. Other lyricists
lack the literary depth required for analysis to be
fruitful. So, why would I spend my time trying to
excavate a shallow playground sandpit when I could
instead look to Lil Wayne, a lyrical Valley of the
Kings?

To devote such time to the large body of
comparatively uninteresting lyrics offered by the rest
of the rap world would be drudgery, and it wasn't my
purpose. My goal in writing the book was to explore
the literary richness of Wayne's lyrics, not to do a
general survey of all rap. But, the callers and others
have clearly expressed an interest in data-driven
comparisons of Wayne's lyrics to other rappers'. This
would require wading through a sea of largely
prosaic, uninspiring lyrics. What do we often do when
we find a voluminous task that's repetitive and
mundane? We get a computer to do it. Fortunately, a
Finnish computer science team has done just that and

offered their data for me to cite in this 2nd edition of <u>The Literary Genius of Lil Wayne</u>.

*Rap Machine*

Eric Malmi of Aalto University in Finland led a team consisting of researchers from Aalto, the Helsinki Institute of Information Technology and the University of Helsinki to create the DeepBeat and RankSVM algorithms, which compose original rap lyrics and together constitute a "virtual rapper" or "rap machine." Along the way, Malmi's team fed their algorithms over a half-million lines of rap from the top 104 rappers (almost 11,000 tracks) to identify the longest polysyllabic rhymes ("multi"s) in rap music. In a new chapter, I cite Malmi, et al.'s data and compare Lil Wayne's rhymes to those of other rappers in further support of my arguments for the uniqueness of Lil Wayne's literary genius in rap music

*A Conversation with Cortez Bryant*

After the release of <u>The Literary Genius of Lil Wayne</u>, numerous media outlets featured the book and reported on its surprising claims about Wayne's unsung literary genius. While, as an author, it pleased me to see my book getting some attention, nothing could've prepared me for the aftermath of what I would see online when I landed in Chicago for an academic conference early one cold, rainy Saturday morning: Lil Wayne WEEZY F @LilTunechi: "Much luv for Professor Kreston Kent!" I knew something big would follow. The next night, I got a call that validated my work in a way that nothing else could.

Fans of Lil Wayne know of his best friend and manager Cortez Bryant, who called me in my Chicago hotel room to share exciting news: Wayne's girlfriend had given him a copy of my book, prompting Wayne to worry Bryant with a rare 3am phone call. Seeing Wayne's number at that hour, Bryant feared an emergency, only to pick up the phone and hear Wayne excitedly raving about the book he was reading.

Cortez went on to tell me that Wayne said reading the book was like looking in the mirror, that I saw things in his lyrics that he was trying to do but that no one else saw. Wayne went on to say that I think the way he does, that I described what he was trying to do in ways he's always known but couldn't articulate himself. Cortez told me that Wayne had been calling him periodically ever since to read him passages of my book. At that point, I didn't care whether my book ever sold another copy; the book had accomplished more than I'd ever hoped. The icing on the cake was a shout out for the The Literary Genius of Lil Wayne: the case for Wayne to be counted among Shakespeare and Dylan on *Sorry 4 The Wait 2*'s "Preach," in which Wayne raps, "too much fucking talent: rap's Shakespeare. Go Hamlet."

[Knowing Wayne had read the book and that he knew I studied at The University of Virginia, I also wonder if the "Cavalier" reference in the same song is not a coincidence. There's also a line in "Sh!t,"–"I'm a nerd; I'm a geek. I'm absurd; I'm unique."–that's reminiscent of a line from the first edition of the book:

7

"both Lil Wayne and Bob Dylan are frequently charged with being opaque, non sequiturian, disingenuous, abstruse, silly, banal, indulgent and nonsensical."]

*Sorry 4 The Wait 2*

Wayne's latest mixtape (as of publication of the 2nd edition) features ingenious use of literary devices that rivals any of his previous work. Thus, this 2nd edition also features a new chapter analyzing highlights from the mixtape.

# Introduction

*Hiding in Plain Sight*

Many who consider themselves intellectually serious laugh at the mention of Lil Wayne, but the laugh is on them: this book will show that those who dismiss Lil Wayne are missing out on a true, rarified master of the English language who continues many of the same traditions as Shakespeare. Those who can't see past Wayne's incessant cursing, drug references and misogyny fail to appreciate a lyricist on par with Bob Dylan (who enjoys the Presidential Medal of Freedom, Nobel Prize nominations and near-universal acclaim by music critics and literary scholars). Rather than receiving deserved accolades for his masterful command of language, Lil Wayne makes headlines in articles such as:

"Music That Makes You Dumb,"
for being the most popular musician at colleges that have the lowest average SAT scores,
(http://musicthatmakesyoudumb.virgil.gr)

and scores among the lowest ranking rappers in:

"The Largest Vocabulary in Hip Hop,"
which reports that he uses fewer unique words than most rappers, i.e. has a smaller vocabulary
(http://rappers.mdaniels.com.s3-website-us-east-1.amazonaws.com).

Despite the severely limited scope and methodological shortcomings of those infographics, they reflect real perceptions about Lil Wayne: that he is a drug-addled, tattooed, dreadlocked clown whose misogynistic, sex-obsessed, gangster lyrics score him popularity only with the least discerning listeners. The paradox of Lil Wayne's literary merit is that those who would appreciate it don't listen to him, and those who listen to him generally don't notice or consciously appreciate Wayne's masterful use of literary devices.

While extremely popular, Lil Wayne is critically underrated and his work cursorily dismissed. In

Complex Magazine's
"The 10 Greatest Rappers of the Last 5 Years"
(http://www.complex.com/music/2013/09/greatest-rappers-of-past-5-years/)

the authors of the article rank Wayne down at number eight of ten: this is a slap in the face for a rapper with the tagline "the best rapper alive." The article singles out the song, "I'm on One," as one in which "Wayne...takes up space" and that the song "would be better without him."

On that track, Wayne is joined by Drake, who rhymes "spot," got," and "shot," and Rick Ross, who rhymes "chest"/"rest", "air"/"wear", "hills"/"thrill", "great"/"eight." Both rappers max out at one- or two-syllable rhymes. Wayne rhymes "dust something" with "bus coming", three syllables, and this is an underperformance for Wayne, who often rhymes seven or more syllables between the ends of lines.

Neither Drake nor Ross employs a single pun; Wayne employs at least four in his verse. Drake drops not a single allusion; Rick Ross: namedrops Marc Jacobs gratuitously. Wayne drops Pat Riley as part of a pun; Swisher Sweets as part of a compound rhyme; pairs Andre the Giant with Mayans (who were known to be among the most petite peoples on Earth, in contrast to the giant); and rhymes "Mazeltov" with "Olive Oyl."

Take a look at that last rhyme: Mazeltov and Olive Oyl. Compare it to spot/got/shot from Drake and chest/rest from Rick Ross. Wayne introduces an arresting pair of words: a Hebrew word paired with the name of a classic cartoon character who was voiced by a Jewish woman, and he does so with great sophistication. Mazel / Olive, and, tov / Oyl; they're so close sonically, that it feels natural to mismatch them: "Mazel Oyl" and "Olive tov." Both are five letters followed by three letters (by syllable and by word, respectively). Both have v's and l's as critical consonants. Surely Wayne was aware that he was contrasting Mayans with Giants. If we grant that, should we not allow for the possibility that he was deliberate in pairing Mazeltov with Olive Oyl?

Could they both really just be fortuitous coincidences? In truth, it doesn't matter: great art is great art whether it is consciously constructed or subconsciously produced. This book argues both that Lil Wayne must be consciously aware of the richness of his literary constructions but also that it doesn't matter whether he is or isn't aware of it: the work stands on its own.

In the same verse, Lil Wayne also employs two or three non-pun jokes, whereas the other two rappers don't make a single identifiable joke. Wayne's verse in "I'm On One" is far from his best work but is also indisputably more meritorious than the other two rappers' verses on the track. Why would Complex Magazine assert that the song would be better without Weezy? Lil Wayne has become a punching bag for rap pundits who react negatively to his ubiquity and propagate the misconception that his lyrics lack substance. It is true that his lyrics lack narrative substance; that's not Lil Wayne's enterprise. However, the lack of narrative in Wayne's songs is more than compensated for by the richness and density of his literary devices. Storytelling is certainly a valuable skill and one that is broadly appreciated; but narrative content alone is neither necessary nor sufficient to constitute literary genius.

The literary analyses in this volume will show that under the veneer of drugs, sex, money, prejudice and violence, Lil Wayne's vocabulary is sophisticated and erudite. It is, in fact, his masterful use of various kinds of literary repetition and his many recurring themes that account for the narrower breadth of words in Lil Wayne's music that was noted by "The Largest Vocabulary in Hip Hop." Lil Wayne rhymes more syllables per line than anyone else in music. In one instance ("Watch My Shoes"), Wayne rhymes fifteen syllables line-to-line. Not only does Wayne offer the longest polysyllabic rhymes in rap, but he also composes them in much more natural language and in combination with other literary devices, whereas the other longest rhymes in rap are forced, choppy, unnatural and lack other literary qualities. Beyond rhyme, Lil Wayne packs literary allusions, metaphors, cultural references and puns into his songs with unrivaled density.

In a Cambridge Forum Radio podcast (2000), renowned scholar Sir Christopher Ricks, one of the world's foremost literary critics, made his case for Bob Dylan's literary greatness by highlighting Dylan's line, "the highway is for gamblers; better use your sense" for its pun on sense/cents and for Dylan's epistrophe in "The Lonesome Death of Hattie Carroll": the repetition of the word "table" at the ends of three consecutive lines to evoke the monotony of her life. However, one can identify more puns in a single Lil Wayne song (try, "I Don't Like," for one) than perhaps in Dylan's entire cannon; and it will be shown that various forms of literary repetition–very much in the same vein as Dylan's "table"–abound in Lil Wayne's songs, bringing new, rich meanings to his words and phrases. For example, in "Live from the 504" (Da Drought 3), Wayne raps, "it's going down, it's going down, like there's a whale in the boat." Setting aside for the moment the pun on "it's going down" and the simile (Polonius: "very like a whale"), the simple repetition of "it's going down" evokes a sailor crying out "it's going down! it's going down! abandon ship!", even though Wayne doesn't mimic that in the delivery at all.

Lil Wayne's literary genius hides in plain sight. The unsavory subjects he expounds upon obscure but do not invalidate the literary merit of his works. Fans of other rappers complain that Lil Wayne's music lacks narrative content and sympathetic character.

However, it is the absence of these aspects that frees Lil Wayne to play so densely and masterfully with the English language: as this book will show, Wayne's songs serve as a playground for his virtuosity with puns, rhyming, allusions, metaphors, humor and structure. And Lil Wayne's music is not devoid of message: through his consistent motifs and themes, Wayne does offer a message; however, one that is often gleaned through exposure to a wide breadth of his work, rather than always being spelled out in a single song. While the casual listener may either embrace or dismiss his music on a visceral level, the attentive listener of Lil Wayne can unlock appreciation and enjoyment of literary genius.

*Scope of the book*

This book argues that Lil Wayne is a genius, that his usage of literary devices sets him apart from other rappers, and that he should be counted among Shakespeare and Dylan as an artist widely recognized to have a masterful command of the English language who brings profundity to his work and elicits epiphanies from his audience. While this book makes note of many instances where Lil Wayne uses particular literary devices, it is not a comprehensive encyclopedia of literary devices in Lil Wayne's lyrics and does not seek to prove its claims beyond dispute. The book will take up the keystone elements of rhyme, repetition and puns as the literary devices in focus, aiming to initiate serious conversation about the artistic merit of Lil Wayne's words and to invite causal listeners, rap aficionados and music critics to stop cursorily dismissing Lil Wayne and instead awake to his literary genius. There is much more to Lil Wayne's songs than first meets the ear.

## Timeline

This text focuses on Lil Wayne's work from 2007 to the present. While his music has progressed through five distinct stylistic periods in that time, it is broadly characterized (save for three albums: Rebirth, Sorry for the Wait and IANAHB2) by an intellectualism not found in his prior efforts, from 1999-2006.

*Da Drought 3, The Leak and Tha Carter III*

This period features facile, dynamic, playful, innovative and melodious vocal delivery styles. Not nearly as dense in puns, polysyllabic rhyme, or other literary devices as his later work but basking in fast-moving imagery, the lyrics of this period are characterized by abundant humor, casual joviality and rapidly shifting metaphorical paradigms.

*No Ceilings*

Featuring a distinctive style all its own, this mixtape stands as the richest example of literary virtuosity in all of rap music. The density, complexity and elegance of Wayne's employment of rhyme, allusions, metaphors, imagery—as well as the album's adumbration of his later infatuation with puns—elevate this mixtape to serve as the pinnacle of Lil Wayne's cannon.

## Post-prison and Carter IV

Lil Wayne's vocal delivery grew stale during this period of forced puns and try-hard cleverness; however, Tha Carter IV still manages some arresting (no pun intended) profundity and some head-scratchers that lead to startling epiphanies once decoded; for example: "I still got da vision like a line between two dots" (from "Blunt Blowin").

## Dedication 4 and Dedication 5

Dedication 4 and Dedication 5 resurrect much of Lil Wayne's talent for dynamic vocal delivery and channel the more organic vocal style of Tha Carter III, while simultaneously featuring a much greater density of puns than prior periods. While IANAHB2 actually falls between these two mixtapes in terms of its release date, its style, which echoes Rebirth more than IANAHB, largely doesn't fit with these vastly superior mixtapes ("Curtains" and "Rich as Fuck" excepted).

## Adumbrating Tha Carter V

As of publication, five tracks have been released from Tha Carter V: "Believe Me," "Krazy," "Grindin," "Gotti," and "Off Day." In these, Lil Wayne sounds energetic and driven, showcasing his literary talents balanced against an aggressive, insouciant style of expression.

# Questions of Authorship

Like Shakespeare's and Dylan's, the authenticity and originality of Lil Wayne's work has been drawn into question. There are serious academics who make convincing cases that William Shakespeare never existed or that he did exist but had nothing to do with writing plays. Each time Dylan has released an album this century, there have been new accusations of plagiarism. There have been reports of brainstorming sessions among Lil Wayne, his producers and his Young Money crew coming up with lines for Wayne's songs. In each case, regardless of the veracity of the charges, the very fact that these accusations exist points to general incredulity that a single person, especially one of modest beginnings and average education, could create such great work. It is a testament to Lil Wayne's literary skill that people feel compelled to search for alternative sources of his work; they simply find it hard to believe that Lil Wayne could exhibit such genius.

Even if Wayne does hold such brainstorming sessions with his colleagues, we recognize that collaboration is part of the creative process and that no artist exists in a vacuum. As President Obama said, "you didn't build that." When he was ill, Mozart hired an assistant to help him finish his musical scores. Picasso collaborated with Braque in the development of Cubism. The most economically successful fine artist of our time, Jeff Koons, has dozens of assistants doing the legwork to realize his ideas, but it's still his name on the works. As president of Young Money Records, Wayne puts creative teams together to produce music. However, this book argues that Wayne's own raps retain a unique literary quality reserved for his voice alone: neither his compatriots at Young Money nor his fellow rappers in the broader scene ever approach the density, complexity, structure, or sophistication of Wayne's raps. This is why people marvel at it; this is why he continues to be the most ubiquitous voice in rap fifteen years into his career; and this is why people have trouble believing that Lil Wayne himself can be fully credited with authorship.

## Lil Wayne, Folk Artist

Among academic types, Bob Dylan is a common favorite. No one looks askance or questions me when I name Dylan as one of my two favorite musical artists. However, when I mention Lil Wayne to my colleagues, I often find myself facing a mouth agape, a scowl, or an expression of disbelief: "that's a joke, right?" Even those who accept my declaration of favor for Lil Wayne often come back with, "Dylan and Lil Wayne? That's an odd combination." But it is not odd; not at all.

First of all, they're both superb lyricists, each with his own distinctive style. Secondly, both Lil Wayne and Bob Dylan are frequently charged with being opaque, non sequiturian, disingenuous, abstruse, silly, banal, indulgent and nonsensical. Finally, both are accused of stealing lines, not just because people seek to tear down those at the top, but also because both are engaged in the folk tradition.

Musically speaking, both Dylan and Lil Wayne use existing songs as scaffoldings on which to construct their own. Dylan draws from country, blues, bluegrass, folk and early rock music, sometimes taking melody, harmony, rhythm and even many of the lyrics from an existing song and putting his own spin on it, inserting his own lines. Wayne raps atop existing tracks from other artists and also samples from older pop and rock songs, especially on his mixtapes. This is a clear extension of the folk tradition, modernized.

Curiously, roughly ten years into each of their careers, both Dylan and Wayne released albums that were viewed broadly as career self-sabotage but that ended up putting hardly a dent in their careers: Dylan's was called Self Portrait, viewed as rambling and lacking cohesion; Wayne's Rebirth, viewed as a sophomoric attempt at Rock.

Both have also shown appreciation for nursery rhymes, with Dylan releasing a whole album, Red Sky, that riffs on the structural forms of nursery rhymes; Lil Wayne draws on the same structural forms and also alludes to existing nursery rhymes (Jack and Jill, for example, in "Cashed Out," which also references other children's characters including Gremlins, Tom and Jerry, Mickey Mouse, Barney and Baby Bop). Lil Wayne's song "Started" begins each verse with the same line, maintains a consistent (although not unbroken) rhyme scheme throughout, essentially consisting of groupings of four lines, like many nursery rhymes, with alternating or coupled rhymes at the ends of lines.

While Dylan pulls lines from antebellum era poets, Japanese novelists, early blues songs and the folk cannon, Wayne pulls lines from Sam Cooke, Paul Simon, Michael Jackson, Nirvana, Green Day, 2Pac, B.I.G., Eminem, Jay Z, as well as movies, television shows, ad campaigns and even the ancient Greek historian Thucydides ("the strong do what they will; the weak do what they must," or, as Wayne put it in "A Milli": "I do what I do; you do what you can do about it."). Lil Wayne's cannon is a compendium of popular culture, colored by his particular viewpoints and synthesized into poetical lyrics. As someone exactly the same age as Lil Wayne, I enjoy a unique appreciation for Wayne's abundant allusions. His musical cannon serves as a distillation of American cultural history from 1982 through the present, including older historical references most relevant to our time.

Even when Lil Wayne steals outright from other rappers, he often improves upon the original. For example, fans of Lil Wayne might have been disappointed to learn that Eminem actually paired "Sarah Palin" with "parasailing" before Wayne did. As always, it can't be known whether Wayne picked it up from Eminem or came up with the pairing independently. But what can be known is who used it better, and, unsurprisingly, the answer is definitively Lil Wayne. Eminem throws the two phrases haphazardly into different relative placements in consecutive, conversational lines of "Taking My Ball." Eminem uses the name without any commentary or connection to the surrounding context of the song. Wayne places "parasailing" and "Sarah Palin" correspondingly at the ends of their respective lines, each fitting within his A/B/A/B', B'/B'/B/B' rhyme scheme of the verse. Moreover, instead of being a completely arbitrary name drop as in Eminem's song, the name Sarah Palin fits within a broader context of meaning: "F," "failing," "dumb," and "Palin" are the ends of the phrases leading up to her name in the song. A similar comparison is evident in the song "My Generation," with Nas, where, as in all collaborations involving Lil Wayne, he puts his colleague to shame...

## Intentionality

Nas ranks in the top few (sometimes first) in all the lists of best rappers on the first two pages of a casual Google search, whereas Wayne doesn't even break into the top 15. Those who consider themselves to be connoisseurs of rap simply don't take Lil Wayne seriously. However, even a quick, rudimentary analysis of the two rappers' verses in "My Generation" shows a wide disparity in their literary quality. In causal conversation, when I have pointed out some of the highlights of Lil Wayne's lyrics to friends, the irrepressible question is always, "yeah, but do you think he knows he's doing that? Was it intentional?"

Nas's verse in "My Generation" features one- or two-syllables rhymes from line to line and a string of "-ation"s with no other mutual resemblance or relevance; Wayne's verse features, 2-, 3-, 4-, 5- and 8-syllable rhymes. Wayne's rhyming lines have thematic ties that augment each other's meanings, and his verse features allusions to important cultural touchstones of the civil rights movement. Compare Nas:

> I reach them like Bono, [six syllables]
> so get rid of your self-sorrow.
> [eight syllables]

to Wayne:

> If you weather that storm, then that
> rain bring sun. [six, five]
> Been a long time comin'; I know
> change gonn(a) come. [six, five]

Nas' syllabic counts don't match: six to eight and his second line uses the cumbersome phrase "so get rid of your." He could've said:

> I reach them like Bono [six]
> so rid yourself sorrow. [six]

Wayne matches the syllabic counts of his phrases and draws on both a weather idiom and a seminal civil rights ballad by Sam Cooke (and later in the verse, "Man in the Mirror"). Nas chooses to rhyme the title word "Generation" with "gentrification," "frustration," and "instrumentation," none of which even have the same number of syllables as "generation." For Wayne's part, he rhymed "generation," four syllables, with "revelations," also four syllables; but further, Wayne even matched the vowels perfectly: both words are -e-e-a-io-. Such attention to detail pervades Lil Wayne's work and simply isn't present in others' raps. The fact that this verse is unexceptional in Wayne's music and that such constructions are the rule rather than the exception for him, suggest either that he does, in fact, intend them, or that his genius manufactures them unconsciously.

Arguably the greatest classical composer, Mozart, may have been somewhat of an idiot savant and may or may not have been consciously aware of the theory behind his music. He composed some of his symphonies on the spot in a single draft without hesitation, premeditation, or revision; did he, in real time, deliberately construct his melodic structures, harmonic progressions and forms? Or did Mozart simply have an ingrained sense of those principles that allowed his genius to produce them almost reflexively? Some experts have argued the latter. Much of Lil Wayne's music is recorded on the spot; however, he is known to go back and revise and revise and revise. The aforementioned brainstorming sessions may or may not be accurate reports. Wayne himself reports having gone through phases of writing his lyrics down in advance and alternately not writing them down at all. Whatever the process, we see the results; and this book aims to convince the reader that the results are impressive from a literary standpoint, and further, impressive enough to constitute a sign of genius.

## What Constitutes Genius?

More than anything else, true geniuses have in
common a compulsion to produce: They're prolific.
Lil Wayne epitomizes this. With over forty albums
and over a thousand songs, Wayne has matched in
only fifteen years what it took Bob Dylan fifty years
to produce. Some of that has been junk, but the junk
does not invalidate the masterpieces. Sheer
probability dictates that with such an output, some
songs are bound to fall short; even Beethoven and
Mozart wrote a few pieces best suited for the waste
bin.

Many acknowledge the cleverness of Lil Wayne's
lyrics but would balk at granting him the
appellation "genius," despite the fact that he's
incredibly prolific. Being prolific may be one indicator
of genius but not sufficient in itself. Perhaps more
people would acknowledge the underlying genius in
Lil Wayne's songs if they saw the broader structural
forms within them. This is difficult to do
when listening, because we only get a linear,
chronological exposition of material as it comes out in
the song. When we hear, for example, a reference
to "she wants cocaine" in the last verse of "Krazy," we
don't remember the reference to Snow White from
the first verse. When we hear a reference to liquor in
the line after "cocaine" in the last verse, we don't
recall the reference to making a toast from the line in
the first verse that followed "Snow White." Parallel
structures like "Ms. Snow White / toast to that" and
"she want cocaine / liquor" are typically opaque to a
listener, especially when separated by two to 4 min.

We can support the notion that Lil Wayne is aware of relationships among the contents of his verses within the song by observing: each verse of "Krazy" begins "Tell me something I don't know"; each of the four verses of the song makes reference to financial constraints (order/bought extra/quota, half off/coupons, treasury/equity/credit, manage/credit/balance), and the first two verses share significant nouns in common with each other ("toast"), as do the last two verses ("credit"). Furthermore, Wayne makes the joke that "we don't name drop," even though he drops the names Snow White and Popeye and brags unabashedly in the song.

We also expect works of genius often to have underlying meaning that isn't readily apparent. There's an undeniable association between the idea of "dropping newborns" (mentioned in "Krazy") and an infamous balcony incident involving a pop star. If we back up from there, we see a line about "school boys"; above that, a line about knocking off half your face. A broader inspection reveals references to: having nothing to prove except in court; giving him something to help him sleep ("the same thing that helped" Martin Luther King sleep when he had a dream, which doesn't happen on Propofol); finding him dancing in the finest mansion; and finally, dying young. Watching the music video (or film) for the song, we see an opening sequence with a man in a crucifixion pose, a staple of Michael Jackson performances as well as a sequence with Lil Wayne wearing two jackets at the same time that are undeniably reminiscent of the BAD and Thriller jackets. Given Wayne's incredible penchant for Michael Jackson references (there's an explicit one in the second single off the same album as "Krazy"), it's not unimaginable that the song is a veiled lamentation or expression of anger about Jackson's death. It would further explain why Wayne, who, like most rappers, incessantly brags about his wealth, would write a song replete with references to financial constraints; without the Jackson reading, that would remain an enigma. This interpretation would also further elucidate the "we don't name drop" remark, i.e. "this song is about Michael Jackson, but I'm not going to drop the name."

[In "D'usse," the song off *Tha Carter V* in which there's an explicit Michael Jackson reference, Wayne pairs MJ with Elvis (both the "King"s of their genres) and also pairs Hootie with Coolio, two stars very much pegged as belonging to the 90's. The importance of <u>pairings</u> in that song is taken up further in the chapter on repetition, below.]

Even if Lil Wayne never intended for the song "Krazy" to be about Michael Jackson, the fact that such an interpretation can be so well supported within the song speaks to how pregnant Wayne's work is, i.e. how much richness there is to be found in it. To be sure, much of the song sounds completely opposed to Michael Jackson's image and lifestyle, but that could be seen as window dressing (to use the phrase loosely) for Lil Wayne fans who expect to hear about his guns, violence, bitches and weed. Since most every Lil Wayne song contains those references, can we not expect that the deeper meaning of his songs might be woven around or behind those obligatory subjects?

In "Started," Wayne raps about reindeers and then mentions noses two lines later. Again, one might at first dismiss the association as coincidental, trivial, or too loose; however, after one recognizes the rhyme scheme of the song and finds "reindeer" and "nose" to be placed in corresponding lines according to the scheme, and after one finds "shooters" and "2Pac" to be in other corresponding places of the same two lines, one might be inclined to believe something is happening here. Furthermore, any noun formed by the suffix 'er' on a verb in the context of reindeers obviously plays on the names of Rudolph's compatriots. Indeed, there are many topics throughout the song paired by their same relative placement in corresponding lines.

The most recent release from *Tha Carter V* (at the time of writing) is "Off Day," a song that many listeners immediately dismissed as excessively vulgar trash and that does indeed, at first listening, sound like it should've remained an unreleased studio farce. However, even this song–featuring nauseating and absurd repetition of "sucking," "fucking," and "cumming"–subtly, perhaps insidiously, showcases Lil Wayne's literary virtuosity.

First, "Off Day" can be considered a fitting bookend if indeed *Tha Carter V* turns out to be Lil Wayne's final studio album (as he asserts), because it references "Back That Azz Up," one of Wayne's very earliest "features" and an enormous hit. The reference serves as an example of Lil Wayne's Folk tendencies, not only because it hearkens back to the older song, but also due to the other cultural allusions Wayne uses to invoke and parallel the earlier song.

In the original song, Manny Fresh alludes to Tweety's "I Tawt I Taw a Puddy Tat." In the cartoons, Tweety and Sylvester always play a game of cat and "mouse." For his own part, in "Off Day," Wayne references **Minnie Mouse** eating cheese<u>cake</u>, and then, a few lines later, in the same place in the line, references **"pussy"** and "<u>frosting</u>": Minnie Mouse and pussy(cat), i.e. cat and mouse.

The frosting cannot but refer back to the cake. Wayne establishes a clear pattern in the song of thematic continuity on alternating lines (not consecutive lines). In the first verse, every *other* line ends: "cake / plate / waist." On alternate lines, he has "she's safe"/"knees scraped." In the same verse as frosting/cake, he has "cheapskate" two lines up from "cheesecake."

Then, in the line following "frosting," he stutters: "buh-buh-buh-begging." Not only is this a pun on "frost"ing, but it's also a play on the incessant stuttering of old cartoon characters of the Tweety/Minnie era.

The verse ends with "my right hand" / "my dice hand" / "like price tag" / "I white flag." If poetry is economy of words (saying much with very few words), as it's often described, then this is poetry:

right hand - obvious masturbation reference
dice hand - shaking motion reinforces ^
"pop that pussy like a price tag," which he'd
probably pull of with his dominant (right)
hand
white flag - price tags are white "flags." dice
are white as well.

Here, "white flag" is not actually used as a noun: the
line is "pop that pussy...'til I white flag." Wayne uses
"white flag" as a verb: "til I white flag," i.e. surrender.
When one surrenders, he erects a white flag: white
popping up, i.e. ejaculation. [Oh, and frosting is
usually thought of as white by default as well, as was
Minnie Mouse's face originally, and cheesecake.]

In the next verse, Lil Wayne drops the corny pun "she
surf that dick like a heatwave." However, if we relate
it to the other sex-act similes in the song, we have
three white-colored phenomena: cresting waves,
cheesecake, and frosting," perfect companions to the
"white flag" metaphor.

There are also some impressive parallel structures to
consecutive lines in the song:

"She **lock** the d<u>oo</u>r, set the alarm
                    and *TE*xt me SHE **safe**.
  I **got** a big-b<u>oo</u>ty bitch with a *Pe*t-ITE **waist**."

and

"tast**id** LIKE *fros*-t<u>in</u>'
  begg**in** MY *par*-<u>din</u>.

## Controversial Content

We expect literary merit to be reserved for venerated forms of expression, not mixtapes and radio waves. Shakespeare and his medium, the theater, are hallowed; but in his own time, Shakespeare was simply writing in the popular form of the day. Shakespeare's plays are replete with vulgarities, even by today's standards, but they're dressed up in an archaic vernacular that we're conditioned to revere. This is the opposite of the phenomenon that masks Lil Wayne's literary merit: when Shakespeare is being vulgar, it sounds erudite; but Lil Wayne's literary gems simply sound vulgar.

The criticism that Lil Wayne only ever raps about those few sordid subjects actually supports the notion of Lil Wayne's literary genius: how has he not run out of things to say about sex, drugs, money, violence and misogyny? In over forty albums and over a thousand songs, Lil Wayne shows no signs of slowing down in expounding upon these limited subjects. How many ways can one say "she gave me a blowjob"? For that matter, how many variations can one make on:

> "Only God can judge me…"
> "Money talks and…"
> "Weezy F. Baby, and the 'F' is for…"
>  School puns
> "Got the world in my hands and…"
> "Life is a bitch/beach…"
> "If they're fly, then I must be…"
> "If it costs to be the boss…"

"Whip it/that like…"
Picture/photo puns

Lil Wayne proves that for a literary genius, the possibilities are limitless: he's been hammering these themes/motifs for fifteen years and continues to build new, masterful confluences of pun, rhyme, simile, metaphor, and literary repetition around them.

Rappers seem to earn the most praise from critics for their storytelling, usually about growing up in the hood with at least one parent who was less than ideal, being out on the streets, selling drugs, getting mixed up in gangs, rocky relationships or simply passing time idly. Lil Wayne favors blowjobs, pussy, cash, abstract violence and self-aggrandizement over such narratives. While those subjects favored by Wayne are also common to most other rap, it is the addition of narrative content that usually earns other rappers praise. Wayne adamantly refuses to engage with such narrative schmaltz; in fact, he makes fun of it. In "The Sky is the Limit," Wayne raps, "when I was five, my favorite movie was the Gremlins..." Were he another rapper, we could easily imagine him continuing the song, "but the real monster was my daddy [his father, not Birdman]." (Yes, other rappers do try to call such things as Gremlins/daddy a rhyme.) Had that been his line, he may have been praised for his authenticity or vulnerability and then been elevated to the top of the critics' rap rankings among those who tell their origin-stories; but no, Wayne continues instead with "ain't got shit to do with this, but I just thought that I should mention." But Lil Wayne is deceiving us: he claims it "ain't got shit to do with this," but it absolutely does; for, he goes on to say: "looking for some divine and a lil intervention / and birds don't fly without my permission." He's rhyming "five" with "divine" and "fly"; and "Gremlins" with "[inter]-ven'shin." The mention of Gremlins is integral to his rhyme scheme. Then he rhymes "permission" with the conflation of the previous two ends of lines, "mention" and "intervention," as if to evoke the word "intermission," which is what occurred when he interjected "ain't got shit to do with this," an intermission, i.e. a break in his rhyme scheme.

Further evidence of Lil Wayne's persistent capitalization on the interplay between words in corresponding places between lines can be found in "Abortion" (from Tha Carter IV). Echoing Dylan's gambler who uses his cents/sense, Wayne raps "Down on the ceiling, looking up at the bed, / life is a gamble, better check the point spread." Get it? Bedspread. (Note: five/six syllables in the first line, five/six syllables in the second line.) Later in the song, Wayne begins a line "Life is..." and begins the next line with "a blessing..." The song's density and richness go well beyond this, and I invite the reader to take a few listens to "Abortion" to experience one of Lil Wayne's greatest compositions.

As in "Krazy," which tempts us to regard Lil Wayne's sex, drugs, violence trifecta as masking something more substantial, "Abortion" peppers its profundity with the banality of the gutter as if to remind us that it's simply the genre in which Wayne works. Perhaps Lil Wayne is reflecting on this tension between the substantial message and literary inventiveness he offers on the one hand, and his vulgarities on the other, when he says "I'm trying to walk a straight line, but the line's crooked." Of course, that line (no pun intended) is immediately preceded by the word "dick," reminding us that he opened the song, "I woke up this morning, dick rock hard." So, what is it exactly that's crooked?

In the same song, Lil Wayne himself best sums up the paradox in his music—the juxtaposition of profundity and vulgarity—when he raps: "I make it [the world] spin on my finger. / I'm a critical thinker" and, of course, adding, for the sake of appearances or perhaps to be true to his artistic self, "I'm a hell of a smoker / and a bit of a drinker."

## Form Over Flow

The most celebrated rappers offer not only narrative (as noted above), but also "flow." The rappers Black Thought, Childish Gambino and Kool G Rap, oft-noted for their polysyllabic rhyming, serve up frequent three-syllable and occasional four-syllable rhymes line-to-line (or within the same line). One can find much less common five, six, or seven syllable rhymes in the rap cannon from those rappers, or Jay Z, or Eminem. A few rappers, including Tech N9ne, Eminem, Slaughterhouse, and others even have taken it further a few times with eight, nine, and ten syllable rhymes. Weezy stands apart, regularly offering 12+ syllable rhymes.

Eminem, T.I., Notorious B.I.G. and MF Doom pack their raps especially densely with rhymes—often much more densely than Wayne—but their rhymes are shorter (much shorter on average and never reach the 15 syllables Wayne has thrown out). All these rappers may rap a relatively high percentage of words in any given line, but the rhyming pair only often contains one, two, three, and more rarely four or five syllables. But Lil Wayne stands in a category of his own, *routinely* (not rarely) offering four- and five-syllable rhymes; often seven or eight; and even up to two fifteen-syllable lines in "Watch My Shoes" (*No Ceilings*) where thirteen of the fifteen syllables from each line match by rhyme.

B.I.G. might have a line of 22 syllables containing a trio of three-syllable words (or phrases) that rhyme, plus another word that rhymes two of the syllables, for a total of 11 rhyming syllables in the line (50%), but that is still only three syllables to each rhyming

phrase (e.g. "scramb[o]ling... gamb[o]ling... mandolins" in "Notorious Thugs"). Wayne can match that, of course, offering up an impressive flow of three-syllable phrases in "Krazy": from "referee" / "credit clean," through "nectarine" / "Grenadine." But Lil Wayne goes much further than that: in "Dough Is What I Got" (*Da Drought 3*), Wayne has a string of five-syllable rhymes: "lame, they call charging" / "same, I'm a Martian" / "brain, I'm retarded" / "Jane, I'm your Tarzan" / "played like (an) accordion." And, in "Krazy" (again), he even has parallel rhymes of 7 and 8 syllables in the opening lines.

The density of rhymes and their rapid-fire succession, combined with the fluidity of delivery and a mellifluous progression of words can be called "flow." While Wayne can hold his own against any rapper in terms of flow, he would be far from the undisputed champion and probably isn't even among the top five or ten. However, when it comes to parallel structure, or "form" (as in the form of a musical composition, e.g. "rondo form," "sonata-allegro form," or, in poetry, a haiku), Lil Wayne has no competition in rap. The formal structure of the verses and parallel structures between lines make Wayne's rap absolutely unique and ingenious from a literary standpoint. Wayne's style of composition doesn't fit within the rap mold, despite the fact that it is rap and is in the hip hop genre: his style of lyrical composition is much more traditional, resembling that of Bob Dylan or others who work in traditional song forms, where the structure of the verses and parallel structures of the lines fit a grand scheme. This is why we have seen, in analyzing Wayne's lyrics, strong interrelationships between lines and verses; and this is how Wayne imbues his lyrics with so much more meaning that first meets the ear.

Of course, such a rapping style as Lil Wayne's—being both unique and also demanding on the listener—turns many people off. Many listeners want to be delighted by a rap upon first listening or to feel intelligent for having picked up on the relationships between consecutive phrases. Wayne makes it difficult. Often, his lines sound like complete non sequiturs, because the connection that's key to the meaning was a few lines up and the listener doesn't have it in mind when the payoff/punchline occurs. This can be perplexing and off-putting for listeners accustomed to lesser demands on their attention spans. For example, the jarring phrase "young dictionary," in "Dough Is What I Got" (Da Drought 3), neither fits the rhyme scheme nor the syllabic pattern of its verse, and, frankly, sounds stupid at first blush, like many of Wayne's "thorn" phrases (see Types of Rhyme, below); however, if rather than dismissing it, the listener sets himself the task of figuring out its role in the meaning of the song, the effort pays off.

In order to understand the meaning of "young dictionary," we must look well beyond its immediate vicinity in the song at the entire structure. "Dough Is

What I Got" is a remix of "Show Me What You Got," and Lil Wayne capitalizes on the play of the "oh" sound. In fact, it's not always clear whether he's actually saying "dough" or simply, "oh is what I got." His first verse begins with "Give a woman none." None. Zero. 'O.' For reinforcement of the "oh" theme, he gives us these lines:

"Got that subzero flow how you want me, Ma?
Make her get over here like Scorpion."

*Got that sub-0 flow...*
*Make her get O-ver here...*

Not only do 0 and O both fall on the fourth syllables of their respective lines, they both even occur after the 10th letter of their respective lines. In a rhyme tied beautifully to meaning and the O-theme, Wayne raps:

"I must be Le**bron** *James* if he's JOR-<u>dan</u> /
No. I **wan'** *rangs* for my per-FOR-<u>mance</u>."
[rings are O-shaped]

Having now established the importance of "o" and "0" in the song, let's take up the question of the odd phrase "young dictionary," which appears in these lines:

"Tell the world take six.
Young dictionary make words make sense."

Wayne says "take six" instead of "take five," meaning he's taking more or he's got plenty to give, so the world can take more. It's also evocative of Victor Borge's "inflationary language." "Six" is paired in the rhyme with "sense," as in "sixth sense." This is followed by "I make cents make dollars," the same sense/cents pun referenced from Bob Dylan above. Turning cents into dollars is inflation (or augmentation), like turning the expression "take five" into "take six." It's also what a C.E.O. is supposed to do, which comes up later in the same verse. Furthermore, when you turn cents into dollars, you add a digit, a '0.'

All of the above fits cohesively but doesn't yet fully elucidate the oddity "young dictionary." Another line that doesn't fit syllabically or in terms of rhyme is "only for me because of who I a.m." (a nice pun on "am" and "a.m. as in, ante meridiem or "morning" as ends the next line). So, the "young dictionary" is "who I a.m.", which is further reinforced three lines down, where Wayne says "the C.E.O.", which, like I.A.M., is a three-letter initialism. Of what is Wayne C.E.O.? Of Young Money. He has the largest vocabulary and most erudite wordplay of the Young Money crew, and it's his job to "make cents make dollars." Thus, he's the "young dictionary."

As a further Bob Dylan comparison, Dylan's "Trying to Get to Heaven" (*Time Out of Mind*) meticulously adheres to a grand structure of parallel verses in which the meanings of corresponding parts across the verses enhance and augment each other like Lil Wayne's do. For example, in one verse, Dylan sings, "I was ridin'...with Ms. Mary Jane...in Baltimore," which we think is a recreational activity until it is followed by, in corresponding place in another verse, "When you think...you've lost everything, you find out you can...lose a little more." Besides the beautiful rhymes "Mary Jane" / "everything" and "Baltimore" / "little more" (note the visual resemblance Mary/every and the 'L', 'T', 'T's of "Balti"/"little"), Dylan communicates desperation, not recreation, by linking the parallel lines across the verses, revealing the true meaning and motivation behind getting high in the song to be the opposite of what it may have appeared to be in isolation.

When analyzing most rap, the traditional tools of literary analysis aren't readily applicable. Much of the rap out there is poetical, but it is not poetry in a traditional sense, primarily because it's myopic: the rhymes occur in close succession and the references/wordplay appear within an immediate vicinity. In order to see rhyming pairs and related wordplay, one must only look within a range of a few words or a couple phrases to see the rhyme and to understand the meaning. This makes sense because the audience receives rap aurally. We can't be expected to keep in mind what was said a full minute ago in order to understand what's being said now, especially without numerous repeat listenings. Rap is typically linear, unfolding in sequence. But this is where Lil Wayne breaks the mold: he structures his lyrics beyond small groupings of words and phrases. Wayne doesn't only give us ideas that relate to the immediately-preceding and immediately-following word or phrase; he offers meanings that can be gleaned by relating a word or phrase to the one that parallels it in a previous line, or two lines up, or in a previous stanza or verse. Lil Wayne composes his verses and lines in structures that become apparent only when you examine the

overall form of the song's lyrics. With respect to this sort of form, has no equal in rap music.

Because of the myopic/linear nature of "flow," we wouldn't call practitioners of it geniuses from a standpoint of literary analysis: flow so often comes out in freestyle, "off the dome," and doesn't require a long attention span to decipher. Literary genius must be more pregnant than that: it must offer longer-term payoff, hard-won epiphanies, and a grander scheme than what pops out of so many rappers' heads. There are a dozen or more rappers out there with exceptional flow. If we call rappers geniuses based on their "flow," there would be too many geniuses, and the word would lose its rarified quality. We might refer to flow itself as a "genius" in the archaic sense of the word, which meant "a highly refined or rarified skill," but to call a skilled practitioner of flow–even the best of them–a "genius" might be a slippery slope. This book argues that Lil Wayne's exogenous approach to rapping distinguishes him categorically from his peers and imbues his lyrics with greater complexity, more layers of meaning, more hidden meanings, and more structural integrity (form) than other rappers, earning him the rarified label of "literary genius," unique to him in the rap world and joined in the broader world of words (or "letters") by Shakespeare and Dylan.

# Rhyme

Rhyming is arguably the most important literary device in rap. It is no accident that "rhyming" (or even "spitting rhyme") is synonymous with "rapping." Almost all rap features rhyming. However, Lil Wayne has taken rhyming to a measurably higher level. While most rappers offer only mono-, di, or maybe tri-syllabic rhymes, Lil Wayne routinely knocks out much higher-degree polysyllabic/multiple rhymes, taken to an extreme with a fifteen-syllable rhyme that appears in "Watch My Shoes" (No Ceilings). Wayne's lyrics cover every documented literary type of rhyme, many of which are noted below. But even more than the superiority of his syllable counts and the diversity of his types of rhymes, Wayne's rhymes play on meaning more than any other rapper's.

It has been shown that Lil Wayne is acutely aware of the connections between words placed in the same relative location in corresponding lines, whether that is beginning, middle, end, or even the specific syllable number in the line. Knowing this, let's look at these lines from "Break Up" (No Ceilings):

"I'm here to distinguish /
the bears from the penguins."

First, we have slant rhyme, assonant rhyme and internal rhyme taking place. But I'm more interested in how the corresponding words between the lines enrich each other's meanings. Let's begin with "here" and "bear." Both words have homonyms: hear, here;

and bear, bare. Would it be overanalyzing to suggest that "I'm here" might play on "eye" and "hear"? For any other rapper, I would say yes. For Wayne, no. Here's why:

In "My Nigga," (YG feat. Lil Wayne), Wayne offers the enigmatic line: "eyes red from the kush I blew: white person." It's clear why his eyes were red, but what does "white person" mean in this context? This is the sort of apparent non sequitur for which people attack Lil Wayne, accusing him of spouting arbitrary words and phrases. "White person" is the typical racial description of most people who have blue eyes, i.e. eyes of blue, i.e. "I blew" (which was set up by the preceding "red" to evoke color when we hear "blew"). Delightfully, Wayne has rhymed "white person" with a preceding line ending in "vice versa," which adumbrated the interchangeability of "I" and "eye"; "blew" and "blue."

Given this, we can imagine that Lil Wayne was pulling something similar in "Break Up" when he says "I'm here." Thus, we can consider the alternative meaning, "eye 'em; hear' to distinguish," i.e. watch and listen in order to distinguish.

We can safely assume that by rhyming "distinguish" and "penguins" at the ends of their respective lines, Lil Wayne is inviting us to reflect on distinguishing penguins or, more likely "distinguished penguins." What would make penguins distinguished? Their well-affirmed association with tuxedos. Now we have "bears" contrasted with tuxedos, or, better, "bares," i.e. the poor unclothed or barely clad contrasted with the wealthy in tuxedos. Or those with the bare necessities vs. those with plenty.

Lil Wayne leaves little doubt about this interpretation, as his next line is "life is just a gap / get some money in between it," continuing the same rhyme, thus linking it to the line in question and affirming the association between distinguishment, bareness, penguins (tuxedos) and money.

But Wayne also offers us further support for the alternative spelling "bare." It's important to note there is no official publication of these lyrics that's disseminated to consumers, thus, the choice of how to transcribe Lil Wayne's words is up to the transcriber. This allows Lil Wayne the freedom to exploit puns without having to print official copies of lyrics containing slashed pairs of words, as in this case: "I'm/eye 'em here/hear to distinguish / the bares/bears from the penguins." So, there's nothing to say that he necessarily meant "bear" over "bare" as the primary spelling, but the pairing with penguin suggests that the primary spelling should be the animal. As for "bare," we look to other lines within the rhyme scheme and find "walk around in her bikini," which has some close parallels with "I'm here to distinguish":

• "I'm here" and "I'm around" are synonymous.

• "Her bikini" and "to distinguish": a bikini is a "two" piece (pun on to/two)

• "Bikinis distinguish the bares from the penguins (think tuxedos)."

Finally, "here" and "bear/bare" don't strictly rhyme; it's a slant rhyme. Let's consider, then, the possibility that the pairing also evokes the possibility of an exact rhyme. If we change "here" slightly to make it strictly rhyme with "bear/bare," we get "hare," another animal, which would give us "hare," "bear," and "penguin." Alternatively, we could spell it "hair" to rhyme it with "bare," which contrasts hairy with bald or bare skinned, which is how girls wear their bikinis. Also, bears have fur/hair; penguins don't (they have feathers).

Yes, it is likely that some of these meanings were not consciously constructed and that only a few or even none of them were intentional; however, we have seen how much care Lil Wayne takes with the structure of his verses; so, why not this one? And even if none of it is conscious or deliberate, the work still stands as sufficiently rich to support such analyses. This simply cannot be done with anywhere near the frequency or to anywhere near the same extent with other, non-Wayne rap; there is too little structure in other rap to withstand the scrutiny.

One of Lil Wayne's most beautiful, poetic lines also plays with the same slant rhyme as "here" and "bear"; this time it's "air" and "here":

"Look up in the air: it's a crow; it's a robin. /
I been here, but my soul is just arrivin'."
("Watch My Shoes," *No Ceilings*)

Not only does this line sound like it could've been pulled straight off of Dylan's *Love and Theft*, but it bears a striking similarity to Shakespeare:

"And dizzy 'tis, to cast one's eyes so low! /
The crows and choughs that wing the midway air."
(King Lear)

The word "choughs" (another bird) is pronounced "chuffs," so though it may look as if it would rhyme with "low" and "crow," it does not, which now brings us back to Wayne. In "Krazy," Wayne raps: "bought extra clips when I dove in." Is there a pun on "dove in" with the bird name *dove*? In the song's rhyme scheme, "dove in," fits with "snowed in / hoe shit / toast with / close with / nose in /close it / clothes pin / rolls with / holes in / drove in / owe him." It's obvious that Wayne is acutely aware of the parallel structure of the endings of his lines in this song. If we look back two lines, where we would have another rhyme with "dove in" if it weren't the first in the sequence, the line ends "four chicks"–women, yes, but also a type of bird. Whereas Shakespeare's bird name looks like it would rhyme with "dove" but doesn't, Wayne's past-tense verb is a homograph with the bird dove but is pronounced differently, and it's placed parallel with "chicks" so that they both do double duty as a bird name.

## Types of Rhyme

Selected examples of Lil Wayne's usage:

## Macaronic
*Rhyming across different languages:*
"Parlez vous france / hot as picante / hot as a zombie (zombay) / "What else can I say?"
 (from "I Told Y'all")
i.e. What else can I say in other languages?

## Wrenched Rhyme and Slant Rhyme
*Rhyming a stressed syllable with an unstressed syllable, inexact rhyme.*
> "L.A." / "Tele. [as in television or maybe ii-TE-lay, as in Italy]"

> (from "30 Minutes to New Orleans")

The 'A.' is stressed in "L.A.," whereas the "TEL" is stressed in "Tele" [or -TElay] Lil Wayne has to mispronounce "Tele" (TEL-ee) as tel-AY to make it an exact rhyme.

## Assonant Rhyme, Spelling Rhyme and Penultimate Rhyme
*Rhyming the vowel sounds, matching spelling, and rhyming the second-to-last syllable.*
 "[Tempur-]Pedic / cleavage / season / meeting / greedy / Ouija"
 (from "It's Good," *Tha Carter IV*)

 Notice the internal spelling rhymes with the vowels: cleav/seas and meet/greed, bookended by non-spelling rhymes Pedic (PEE-dic) / Ouija (WEE-jee)

## Broken Rhyme

*Rhyming one word with more than one.*
"And stand over ya / arachnophobia"
("Burn," *Dedication 4*)
"Animal / ran a mile" ("Guess Who's Back," SQ4)
 "tourists / would bitch" ("It's Good," *Tha Carter IV*)
"Murk one of these niggers / get earthworms on me
nigger." ("D'usse, *Tha Carter V*)


Lil Wayne also extends beyond broken rhyme to
rhyming a single word with a cluster of words, the
amalgamation of which approximate the original
word, when in the song "I'm Raw", he rhymes the
non-word "comparising" with the cluster of words
that follow: "kerosene, carousel,
parasail,...everything." He has distributed the sound
of "comparising" across four words. In these lines, as
with his entire career, Wayne juxtaposes the
appearance of idiocy (a silly sounding non-word) with
literary sophistication. It's evocative of Shakespeare's
"odious savors sweet" (*A Midsummer Night's Dream*),
when Bottom means to say "odorous." The "odious"
not only invites us to laugh at the character, but also
causes us to ponder the meaning of the slip. The
casual listener might be turned off by Lil Wayne's
apparently random spouting of non-words and words,
but the astute listener of Lil Wayne asks the question,
"why did he use a made-up word, 'comparising'?" If
we give Wayne the credit he deserves, we're rewarded
by discovering that, far from idiocy, Lil Wayne is
constructing something far grander than the one- or
two-syllable rhymes of his peers. In fact, the rhyme
doesn't stop with "everything." Four lines later in the
song, Lil Wayne is still capitalizing on the same move

with "Picasso couldn't paint a better scene." We get the sounds of "parasail" and "carousel" in "Picasso couldn't paint" (notice the internal and spelling rhymes there) and "kerosene" is echoed by "scene." Wayne has even used the homonym "seen" in an intervening line, so then we have three different spellings for the (kero)sene/seen/scene sound (rich/homonym rhyme).

## Vowel pronunciation
*Rhyming different written vowels when they make the same spoken sound.*
"faggot / potato salad"
(from "It's Good," *Tha Carter IV*)

faggit / sallid.

## Scarce Rhyme
*Rhyming words that don't have or have only a few rhyming partners available in the language.*
"thick and red / Ralph Lauren spread / porn star in bed / spar in bed / orange-red /foreign-head / thoroughbread."
(from "Wayne on Me," *No Ceilings*)

In grade school, I was told there was no word to rhyme with "orange."

## Rhyming with the names of letters
*Spelling words and rhyming their spoken letters with full words.*

• In "Demolition Freestyle Pt. 1,"
from Guddaville, Wayne spells G-I-A-N-T
and rearranges the letters into S-A-I-N-T, not only

rhyming words with letters in the process, but rhyming phrases, tying meanings together, and transitioning imagery.

• In "I Told Y'all," Wayne spells out words more rapidly than I can follow, carrying the same delivery, timing, and cadence into the words he pairs to the letters.

• In one of his boldest uses of studio time, Wayne recites the entire alphabet on "Ransom."

## Mispronunciation
*Deliberately mispronouncing a word to rhyme it.*
"I been at Miami water [WOAH-dah] / I'm like a Florida marlin [MOH-lan] / But I come from New Orleans [OH-lans]"
(from "Hustlin," *Dedication 2*)

"Cleaned / everything / medicine (med-i-seen) / Grenadine"

and

"Coupons / newborns [new-bons]"
(from "Krazy," *Tha Carter V*)

## Mispronuncing then correcting
*Deliberately mispronouncing then correcting pronunciation to link two different rhymes.*

"Hollering [hollin'] / Nylon [nylin] / Oops! I mean nylon / pylon."
(from "Run This Town," *No Ceilings*)

and

"Fax machine / Asinine [a-sin-neen] / Oops! I mean asinine / I'm dapper, dime."
(from "You Ain't Got Nuthin," *Tha Carter III*)

## Internal Rhyme
*Rhyming the middles of words.*
"swagger unofficial / maggot on a tissue"
(from "Swag On (Remix)")

The spelling is the same for the first words and the 'c' sounds the same as the 'ss.'

## Progressive Rhyme
*The sound changes smoothly and gradually as the lines progress.*
"symphony / symmetry / sympathy / olympians"
(from "Same Damn Tune," *Dedication 4*)

The middles of the words get progressively harder-sounding.

## Identical Rhyme and Rich/Homonym Rhyme

*Rhyming a word with itself, and rhyming homonyms.*

"I wish you would, nigger.../throw your...body in the woods, nigger."

   (from "Wish You Would," *Dedication 4*)

The identical rhyme is "nigger" with "nigger," a common identical rhyme for Lil Wayne, along with "bitch." Rich rhyme: "would" and "wood."

   Also,

   "I can say don['t] rhyme / and it's gonn(a) rhyme."
   (from "Grew Up a Screw Up," *Lil Weezy Ana Vol. 1*)

## Apocopated Rhyme

*Rhyming the last syllable with the penultimate (second-to-last) syllable (or vice versa).*

"She give me good brain / like she studied at Cam[caim]bridge."
(from "Ice Cream," *No Ceilings*)

Weezy continues later in the song, "...I'm fresher than a Degree [college degree] stick." Perhaps meaning "choose me over a college dude," which would objectify men as "sticks" the way men sometimes have objectified women as "slots."

## Thorn line and Eye/Spelling Rhyme
*Breaking the rhyme scheme with an unrhymed line.*
"Real niggers don't w(h)ine / I'll burn down your vineyard."
  (from "D'Usse," *Tha Carter V*)

The rhyme scheme would have called for a rhyme here, but instead we get the non-rhyming "w(h)ine" and "vineyard"; however, there is an apocopated spelling rhyme here, where the last syllable, "whine" is matched with the second to last (penultimate) syllable, "vine" by sight/spelling but not by pronunciation.

## The Longest Rhyme

*This chapter draws on data provided to me by Eric Malmi, et al., researchers from Aalto University in Finland, the Helsinki Institute of Information Technology and the University of Helsinki, whose paper on computer generated rap lyrics, "DopeLearning: A Computational Approach to Rap Lyrics Generation" can be found at:*
*http://arxiv.org/abs/1505.04771*

*While the published paper ranks Weezy 31st among rappers in the category of "rap density," I have argued at length in the above chapter, "Form Over Flow," how that metric describes— not literary genius, but—only what is commonly referred to as "flow," at which Wayne holds his own but is not the best of the best.*

As I have written, Lil Wayne offers the longest polysyllabic rhyme in rap music with these lines from "Watch My Shoes":

> "Call my nigga Gudda if you tryina get your family back. / [15 syllables]

> All up in anotha nigga' woman I'll be rammin' it." [15 syllables]

According to the Finnish researchers' computer algorithm's search of over a half-million lines from the top 104 rappers, the next longest rhyme comes from Tech N9ne's "It's Alive":

> "Six six triple eight forty six ninety nine three. We back. / [14 syllables]
>
> Sick with nickel plates whorey chicks mighty mine be. We pack." [14 syllables]

While Tech N9ne's offering rhymes the vowels more exactly, it is forced: merely a string of numbers followed by fragmented phrases with little cohesion. Wayne's lines are complete sentences and coherent thoughts.

The next longest rhyme found by the algorithm, weighing in at 13 syllables, comes from Eminem's "White America":

> "But Shady's cute. Shady knew Shady's dimples would help. / [13 syllables]
>
> Make ladies swoon. Baby ooh, baby! Look at myself." [13 syllables]

While this effort is more coherent and has more thematic continuity than Tech N9ne's, Eminem also falls desperately short of Wayne's natural eloquence, rhyming "Shady"/"baby" twice, and needing four sentences plus an exclamation rather than two complete sentences to accomplish the feat.

Other rappers who offer long polysyllabic rhymes are: Jedi Mind Tricks (11 syllables), Sage Francis (11 syllables), AZ (10 syllables), and a number who offer a 9-syllable rhyme or two: Slaughterhouse, The Game, Sage Francis, E 40, Fabolous, Shai Linne, Royce Da 5'9", Nas, MF Doom, Kanye West, Inspectah Deck and Ice Cube.

In sum, there are about 46 polysyllabic rhymes of 9 syllables or longer out of the over half-million lines fed to the computer. [*While the algorithm listed 382 such rhymes, most of those are false-positives whereby a lower-syllabic-count rhyme is repeated; for example, a string of 3-syllable rhymes repeating the same pattern three times would show up as a 9-syllable rhyme in the list. I reviewed the top 50 listed by the computer, out of which 6 were not false positives. At that rate, about 46 out of 382 would be valid.*]

Given the tremendous volume of rap music analyzed, seeing only roughly 46 instances of polysyllabic rhymes 9 syllables or longer means they are extremely scarce. Sixteen belong to Lil Wayne. This means that out of the given data set of 104 rappers, Lil Wayne is responsible for more than one-third of all long "multi"s in rap music! (And this data set doesn't even include *Sorry 4 The Wait 2*, in which Wayne piles on more than a DOZEN rhymes 11 syllables or longer.) Furthermore, Lil Wayne composed the single longest rhyme, weighing in at a hefty, unbeaten 15 syllables that also is neither forced in construction nor fragmented like the closest competitors. Lil Wayne is clearly the undisputed heavyweight champion of polysyllabic rhyming in rap music.

*(Coming in second is Tech N9ne with both the second-longest rhyme and the second-most polysyllabic rhymes in the list: nine of the 46, about one-fifth of the total. Together, Wayne and Tech N9ne have more than half the long "multi"s in rap. Though technically proficient with polysyllabic rhyming, Tech N9ne, beyond having shorter and less frequent long "multi"s, also lacks the literary device usage that Wayne employs.)*

# Repetition

Literary devices serve their maximal purpose when they, as the manner of expression, enrich the meaning beyond that of the words being used. For example, Christopher Ricks cites (Cambridge Radio Forum podcast, 2000) Dylan's description of William Zantzinger's parents as "rich, wealthy parents," which embodies the excess of their wealth by its excess of words, its deliberate redundancy. The words themselves communicate nothing more than the fact of wealth or being rich, but the fact of using both synonyms together in succession draws attention: the anomaly–the apparent superfluity of the synonym as an excess in itself– communicates a potentially culpable excess of money in the hands of the family.

Lil Wayne employs literary devices in the same way, but with much greater frequency than Dylan. For example, in "D'usse," Wayne says, "I only have two goals, and that is: get money, get money." There are two grammatical anomalies in this sentence: the antecedent/pronoun plural/singular mismatch and the omission of the conjunction (asyndeton). The mismatch of tense goals/is (rather than goals/are) flows out of the rhymed pair in preceding lines. "Goals" follows its rhyming partner, "nose." The nose is both singular and dual: one organ consisting of two nostrils. The two goals are one and the same: "get money." The repetition communicates its importance and its extent. Lil Wayne's manner of expression uses fewer words but communicates much more than would something like: "I only have one goal, and that is get a lot of money." To communicate more meaning in fewer words is what we call poetry. Such economy of language draws us back to the masterful repetition of the phrase "I'm me" in Wayne's song of the same name from The Leak.

The deliberate inconsistency of tense (goals/is) evokes Dylan's irregular choice of "which" over "that" in the song "Idiot Wind" (*Blood on the Tracks*). Deliberate grammatical errors or irregularities catch one's attention and alert the listener to the presence of the greater meaning behind the words, the mass of ice beneath the visible surface of the iceberg (a metaphor this book argues applies to Lil Wayne's lyrics). In "Idiot Wind," Dylan sings "it was gravity which pulled us down," and repeats that phrasing in the next line. Not only would "that" be grammatically preferable, but it would also sound much smoother in the song. Why would Dylan choose the more cumbersome "which"? Well, because the song is about a horrible woman, a "witch." The song employs second-person throughout; so, we can re-hear Dylan singing to his ex, "it was gravity, witch [addressing her], ' [that] pulled us down."

[As an aside, Dylan's "Idiot Wind" contains some of the most subtle but simultaneously acerbic and venomous language in popular music. For example, "I can't feel you anymore; I can't even touch the books you've read." But equal to the task is Lil Wayne, who, in "Sex in the Lounge," offers up his own veiled vitriol: "If you're scared, go to church; it's open Sunday."]

The repetition of the choice of "which" over "that" in consecutive lines of the song, combined with its grammatical irregularity, catch the astute listener's attention in the same way that Wayne's tense-disagreement, repetition, and asyndeton pique the analytic ear.

Wayne pulls a similar punch in "It's Good" (*Tha Carter IV*): "gimme three wishes; i wish, i wish, i wish you would," but this is just playful and doesn't, as far as I have discerned, augment the meaning much. We get some more effective humor when Lil Wayne spouts "I can say 'fuck' one time, fuck one time, fuck one time, fuck one time" ("30 Minutes to New Orleans") or when he adds another "get money" later in the song "D'usse," making it three, not two goals; but this time, it's "I might get money." Since when does Lil Wayne express in his songs a lack of confidence about moneymaking? When he wants to draw our attention to the phrase, perhaps inviting us to see the humor.

Wayne's playfulness with repetition manifests as well in his penchant for delivering the same line twice with different timing, intonation or vocal style:

"Show me my opponent. /
[chomp chomp chewing sounds, now talking as if with mouth full:] show me my opponent."
(from "Stuntin' Like My Daddy")

"Take that / no, better yet like Diddy / [doing Diddy impression:] 'Take dat."
(from "You Ain't Got Nuthin," *Tha Carter III*)

"I can kill'em with three lines. / Watch this... / With... / Three lines..."
(from "Grew Up a Screw Up," *Lil Weezy Ana Vol. 1*)

"...like parched throat: ah[em]-ah[em]-ah[em], excuse me"
("Krazy," *Tha Carter V*)

or when he repeats part of a word within another word as in:

"I'm trying to get these 'demons' out of my 'demons'tration"
("Wish You Would," *Dedication 4*)

"Just call me little Carter or little Cardiac [Cart(er)iac]"
("Last of a Dying Breed," from Ludacris' *Theater of the Mind*).

"These hoes are all alike: they put the 'ho' in 'homonym'."
("Bang Bang Pow Pow," T-Pain feat. Lil Wayne)

"I took the 'star' out of starvation."
("Gotti," *Tha Carter V*)

Lil Wayne reverses this form of repetition in "Blunt Blowin'" (*Tha Carter IV*) by inserting additional words into the middle of a phrase, in the same way as Roald Dahl's "scrum-diddlyum-ptious" or in the vernacular, "fan-fucking-tastic; Wayne's version of this: you'll need a "bus pass," then he'll "<u>bus</u>t your <u>ass</u>."

I'll conclude the discussion of Lil Wayne's use of literary repetition with examples of his use of a particularly venerated form of expression, antimetabole, whereby the order of a phrase is reversed upon repetition. Former President Bill Clinton used antimetabole when he said at the 2008 D.N.C. Convention that people have always been more impressed by the power of our example than by examples of our power. These are some of Lil Wayne's antimetabole:

"I'm way high on the highway" ("I Don't Like," *Dedication 4*)

"Don't need another one, when we have one another." ("Popular," *I Am Not A Human Being*)

"Stand under me, 'cus you don't understand me." ("6 foot, 7 ft." *Tha Carter IV*)

"They tell me think it over and I end up overthinking." ("Wish You Would," *Dedication 4*)

## Puns

While it would be difficult to verify empirically, it seems like a reasonable assumption that Lil Wayne has more puns in his body of work than anyone, ever. Even Lil Wayne's nickname is a pun: known as "Weezy," in part due to his grainy vocal delivery style presumed to result from his smoking habits, Lil Wayne hails from Louisiana, or Lou-Weezy-ana. It would be sufficiently impressive, if not ingenious, were Lil Wayne simply to employ puns with the frequency he does, but Wayne goes much further, using puns to link ideas while also fitting the expression of those ideas into polysyllabic rhymes. The confluence of pun, progressions of meaning, and rhyming, woven together seamlessly and succinctly, distinguishes Lil Wayne as a true literary genius.

A common motif throughout Wayne's work is the pun on "give you time," as in allow some time, and as in a judge's sentencing. Bob Dylan employed the same pun masterfully in "Joey" (Desire), "What time is it?" / "five to ten" / "that's just what you get." One of this pun's many incarnations in Wayne's work is "she says, 'give me some time,' /... 'okay, I'm your honor" in which the second line puns on "honor" as well: the judge, she's honored to be with him or vice versa, and even perhaps he's "on her." In the same song, Wayne raps, "that's neither here nor there," an idiom, followed by "she been contemplating short hair," which, again, the casual listener might see as a non sequitur but the careful listener will realize makes perfect sense: short hair doesn't sway *this way and that* and doesn't fall *here and there*: it's "neither here nor there."

In the song "It's Good" (*Tha Carter IV*), Wayne serves up an exceptionally layered pair of puns:

"It's better to give,
but we don't give a fuck about 'em."

Here, we have "better to give" than to receive, sexually, as well as give as in gifts; followed by: "don't give a fuck," as in don't care, but also as in *not giving sexually (a fuck)*, referring back to the expression "it's better to give than receive." Further, this line is preceded by the remark "swimming in the money"; thus, "it's better to give" refers to philanthropy or charity that won't be given because "we don't give a fuck about 'em."

## A few more standout puns:

"I'm not positive I'm definite." i.e. not H.I.V. positive (from "I'm Me," *The Leak*)

"I'm at the bank...call me Mr. Withdrawls. /
I'm with a bitch...call her Ms. Without Draw(er)s"
(from "Hustlin," *Dedication 2*)

"I ain't Santa Claus, but I make it rain, dear."
Reindeer.
(from "Whip It," *Tha Carter III*)

"I should prob'ly see a shrink /
but I'm afraid he'll make me little."
("Devastation," *Dedication 5*)

"I don't see nobody, see no body like a headshot."
("Welcome to My Hood")

By definition, a pun employs a double meaning. Lil
Wayne uses puns to link ideas together with a
single word: the antecedent thought drawing on the
first meaning of the word, with the following thought
drawing on the second meaning of the word. At his
best, the two lines also rhyme, as here:

"ain't promise(d) tomorrow [to-MAR-ah]
...like Nomar Garciaparra."

the promise/Nomar rhymes internally, and to-Mar-
ah clearly rhymes with Garciaparra, but what is the
relationship in meaning that links the lines and where
is the pun? The weaker and less likely pun is that a
common way to phrase that is "you won't see another
day," Gar-SEE-a-parra. The stronger and much more
likely pun is that to not be promised tomorrow means
that there will be no more: Nomar.

# Coda: Sorry 4 The Wait 2

In *Sorry 4 The Wait 2*, Lil Wayne begins and ends with incredible polysyllabic rhyming ("multi"s), opening the mixtape with 12-syllable rhymes in "Coco," following that with an astounding string of 12-syllable rhymes in "Sh!t," further 11-syllable rhymes in "No Haters" and closing with a string of 11-syllable rhymes in "Dreams and Nightmares," all of which would rank among the previous list of the top 6 longest rhymes ever in rap music (as shown in *"The Longest Rhyme"* chapter above). Out of a half-million lines analyzed by the computer (not including *Sorry 4 The Wait 2*), only six of them were eleven syllables or longer; with this mixtape, Wayne adds over a dozen more. Thus, in a single album, Lil Wayne doubles the other 103 top rappers' lifetime output of long rhymes (11+ syllables).

Here are some other literary device highlights from the mixtape, most of which feature multiple literary devices working together in the same phrases. Such layering, richness and depth is characteristically Wayne and uncharacteristic of other rappers.

## No Type: Repetition, Pun, Phoneticization

*While it might be tempting to call this onomatopoeia (everyone's favorite literary-device word), it is not. Onomatopoeia describes an existing, real word that sounds like what it means. "Dick," even repeated six times does not MEAN shaking or electirc chair. Dick means penis. When it is repeated as such, it sounds as close as language can sound to the noise created by an electrocution via "the chair." Thus, we have a phoneticization of the sound combined with a pun, not onomatopoeia.*

"I got her shaking on this dick-dick-dick-dick-dick-dick like an electric chair."

## No Type: **Broken Rhyme, Allusion**
*Perhaps the most artistic broken rhyme ever, using the rhyming phase to describe the name reference spot-on.*

"Bad bitch on my team / just like Katniss Everdeen"

## No Type: **Broken Rhyme, Allusion, Polysyllabic Rhyme**
*Ten-syllable rhyme.*

"She pretty like The Bride of Frankenstein. / She kill it like she married to the mob."

"Pretty like The Bride of Frankenstein" isn't exactly a compliment. Yet, the song is meant to be a homage. Normally, we would expect "pretty like The Bride of Frankenstein" to be an insult, but it has to be sincere in the context of the song. So, what's going on here? The key to understanding this line comes from a broader survey of the song, where we see references to the electric chair, "she kill it," and her suicide note. There's an obvious theme of death in the song. Frankenstein and his bride were both risen corpses. Thus, "pretty like The Bride of Frankenstein" means "drop dead gorgeous." Given that "she" in the song is codeine, which almost killed Lil Wayne before he quit it, "drop dead" gorgeous is especially apt.

## Sh!t: Simile, Pun, Imagery

"Like that blunt between my two fingers I'm at peace."

## Sh!t: Mispronunciation Rhyme

"nylon… / …cayenne [KAI-ahn]."

Wayne has previously (as noted in the "*Rhyme*" chapter) mispronounced and then corrected "nylon" for a rhyme. Here, it's the other word he mispronounces.

## Sh!t: Repetition, Metaphor

"I guarantee no guarantees / but repeat what you heard, you're a dead parakeet."

Wayne repeats the word "guarantee" and warns his competitors against doing the same by threatening they'll be dead parakeets, an animal known for repetition/aping.

## No Haters: Pun

"I want you dead by tonight: that's a real deadline."

A horrible "groaner" of a pun. Deadline / "dead" line, i.e. a line of a song having the word "dead" in it.

## No Haters: Broken Rhyme, Polysyllabic Rhyme

*Eleven-syllable rhyme between these lines.*

"catch a body… / …catastrophic."

## <u>Hollyweezy and Coco</u>: Pun, Motif, Allusion

*Wayne carries this motif – movie-script/lines (pun on script lines and lines of coke)/real or true vs. movie – between two songs on the album.*

HollyWeezy: "Oscar…Golden Globe..ain't no movie, this is real…don't need a script…I know my role…my…bitch just overdosed…snort more coke than Pinocchio."

Coco: "Coke got her all exuberant. She doin lines like a movie script, but these are true events."

## <u>Coco</u>: Extended Metaphor, Polysyllabic Rhyme

"I found a needle in the haystack; put the thread through. /

I tried to stich the wound back up, but I just bled through."

## <u>Coco</u>: Motif, Imagery, Broken Rhyme

"I just want my money. Ain't gotta hold no conversation, no more 'I love you's."

"It's compensation over conversation. / Lord, I must got blurry vision: a nigger's got two        faces."

If your vision were blurry, you probably couldn't distinguish between the printed words "compensation" and "conversation." When you have blurry vision, you see double.

## P.S.

A unique and powerful metaphor–that speaks to love, heartbreak and ingratitude–snuck past me when I was writing the first edition. It's from the song "Grindin" (*Tha Carter V*):

> "Picking up a feather from a lovebird
> is like a medicineball to that bitch."

25241749R00042

Made in the USA
Middletown, DE
22 October 2015